MULTICULTURAL FOLKTALES
AND
ACTIVITIES

Vicki Tyler

D1532613

Troll Associates

Metric Conversion Chart

1 inch = 2.54 cm
1 foot = .305 m
1 yard = .914 m
1 mile = 1.61 km
1 square mile = 2.6 square km
1 fluid ounce = 29.573 ml
1 dry ounce = 28.35 g
1 ton = .91 metric ton
1 gallon = 3.79 l
1 pound = 0.45 kg
1 cup = .24 l
1 pint = .473 l
1 teaspoon = 4.93 ml
1 tablespoon = 14.78 ml

Conversion from Fahrenheit
to Celsius: subtract 32 and then
multiply the remainder by 5/9.

Interior Illustrations by Diana Magnuson

ISBN: 0-8167-3270-1

Printed in the United States of America
10 9 8 7 6 5 4 3 2 1

CONTENTS

INTRODUCTION

Traditionally, folktales have been used to teach timeless values such as friendship, cooperation, common sense, courage, and concern for others. Reading multicultural folktales is a great way to introduce children to diverse cultural backgrounds and to build mutual understanding and respect among people of different backgrounds.

Multicultural Folktales and Activities includes retellings of twenty folktales from Asia, Africa, Europe, North and South America, the Middle East, and the South Pacific. The stories feature a rich variety of heroes and heroines—both human and animal—of different ages, abilities, and backgrounds. Each two-page folktale can be read aloud to younger students or reproduced for older children to read by themselves.

The activities described after each story give you plenty of ideas for building cultural awareness through enjoyable games, arts and crafts, music, and ethnic recipes. Many of these ideas are on reproducible sheets you can duplicate and hand out to each student. Each story has one or two reproducible activity sheets to add to children's learning and enjoyment of the tale.

In addition, you'll find ideas for creative writing and dramatizations to help you integrate the stories into your language arts program. Students are asked to write new endings, create new characters, and imagine new dialogue. They are also encouraged to experiment with writing their own tales and fables on a given theme.

Some activities promote thinking skills such as problem solving, predicting, and comparing and contrasting. Others present opportunities for cooperative learning. Whenever appropriate, projects that link elements of the story to the science or social studies curriculum are suggested. Throughout, students are encouraged to share their own responses, experiences, and customs.

You'll probably think of many other ways to integrate these wonderful multicultural folktales into your lessons. However, the main object of *Multicultural Folktales and Activities* is to introduce your class to the sheer pleasure of stories that have been handed down for many generations by people all over the world.

THE YOUNG HEAD OF THE FAMILY

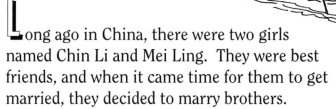

Long ago in China, there were two girls named Chin Li and Mei Ling. They were best friends, and when it came time for them to get married, they decided to marry brothers.

"That way," Mei Ling said, "we can live in the same house and stay friends."

You see, in those days, a boy who got married lived with his father and mother. His new wife would just move into his parents' house with him. So Mei Ling and Chin Li went to live in the house of their husbands' family in a town far away from where they had grown up. They got very homesick.

"Please let us go visit our own families in our hometown!" they kept begging their husbands' father. But the father always said no.

Finally, the father said, "You can go on one condition. Each of you must promise to bring back a gift for me. One must bring fire wrapped in paper. The other must bring the wind wrapped in paper. If you go and cannot find these things, you can never come back."

"That ought to scare them out of going," the father thought. But he was wrong. The girls were so eager to see their families that they were ready to promise anything.

So Mei Ling and Chin Li set off on their long walk home. But on the way, they started to worry. "We'll never find what he wants," they cried. "It's impossible. What are we going to do?"

Just then a local girl named Yingt'ai came riding by on a water buffalo and asked why they were crying. When the young brides explained,

Yingt'ai said, "Don't cry! I know what to do. One of you can bring back a paper lantern. When the candle inside is lit, you will have fire wrapped in paper. The other can bring back a paper fan. When you shake the fan, it will be the wind wrapped in paper." The young brides were overjoyed to hear these wonderful ideas. They thanked Yingt'ai and went on to have a happy visit with their families.

Soon the brides returned to the house of their husbands' family. Mei Ling carried a paper lantern, and Chin Li carried a paper fan. When they showed the father his presents, he was amazed that they had solved his impossible problem. They told him about Yingt'ai, the girl who had helped them, and the father said, "I must ask this clever girl to be the wife of my youngest son!"

So Yingt'ai and the youngest son were married. The father was so pleased with Yingt'ai's wisdom that he made her the head of his family, the one who made all the important decisions. Her decisions were so wise and made the family so happy that the father put up a sign over their house that said "No sorrow." And everyone who passed by was amazed to see a family with no sorrow and a family with such a young and clever leader.

• •

GRADES K-3

Paper Wonders Challenge students to test their wits by solving riddles about paper. How can you carry water in paper? (Make a paper cup.) How can you wear a piece of paper? (Make a paper hat.) How can you scare someone with a piece of paper? (Make a mask.)

Signs of Life The father made a sign saying "No sorrow." Invite students to express their feelings in a sign on poster board or butcher paper. Have them decide what feelings to express. ("We're glad it's spring.") They can work together on the letters and design.

Bright Ideas In the story a young person was able to solve an impossible problem. Encourage students to be problem solvers. Have them suggest how to solve classroom problems. Prompt them by asking questions such as, "How can everyone get a chance to play a game?"

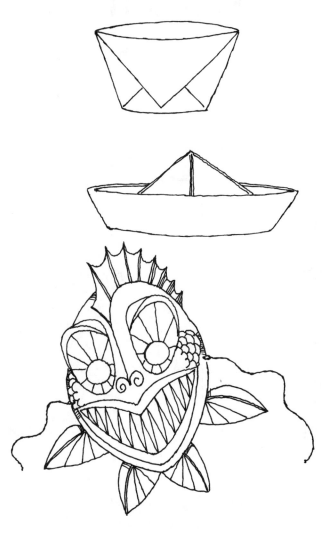

GRADES 4-6

Shaking the Homesick Blues The young brides were homesick. Ask students to imagine they are friends of the girls. What advice would they give? (Bring a treasured item from home, write a letter, etc.) Ask why being homesick was worse long ago than it is today (no telephones or modern transportation).

Words of Wisdom Most cultures have sayings called *proverbs* that give advice. Give students an example of a proverb (e.g. *The early bird gets the worm*.) Have them explain these Chinese proverbs:
When wings are grown, birds and children fly away.
Every day cannot be a Feast of Lanterns.

• •

Wrap the Wind in Paper

Color the Chinese fan. Then cut it out and fold back and forth on the dotted lines. You can wrap a cool wind in a sheet of paper by moving the fan back and forth!

Carry Water in Paper

In the story, Yingt'ai figured out how to carry fire in paper. You can carry water in paper!

1. Cut out the square below.
2. Fold the square in half along the dotted line marked 1. You will have a triangle.
3. Now fold on the line marked 2 and then on the line marked 3.

4. On the line marked 4, fold the top sheet only toward you. Fold back the triangle left on top.
5. If you want, color a design on your cup while it is flat.
6. Now open up your paper cup. Enjoy!

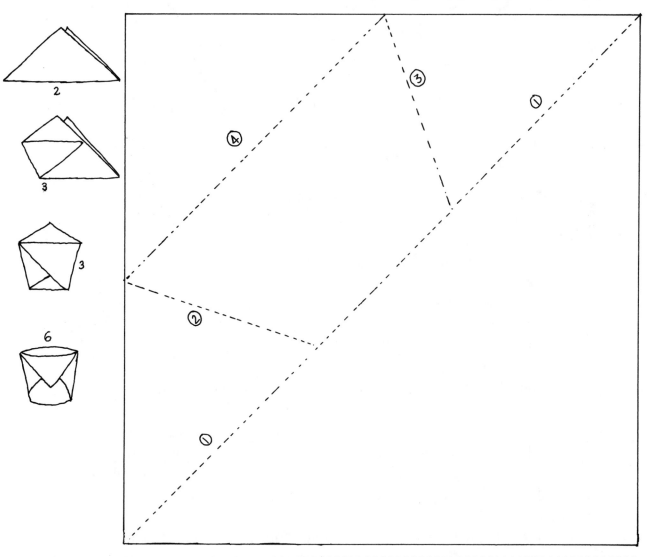

THE STONECUTTER

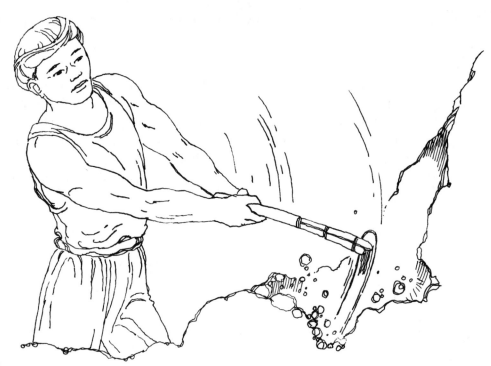

Once there was a man whose job was to cut big slabs of rock so that people could use them to build houses. Every day he went to the side of a mountain and pounded with his tools until big chunks of rock came loose. It was a hard job, but he was very good at it, and he felt happy with his life. For a while.

Then one day he took some stone to a rich man's house and saw all the beautiful things the rich man owned. "Why can't I have such beautiful things?" he complained. "Why do I have to work so hard? Oh, I wish I were a rich man! *Then* I'd be happy!"

And a helpful spirit that lived in the mountain said, "Your wish will come true."

When the stonecutter got home, his little house had turned into a palace filled with servants. And he was very happy. For a while. But one day he looked outside and saw that the sun was drying up all the plants in his garden, and he said, "The sun is so powerful! If I could be the sun, *then* I'd be happy."

And the spirit of the mountain said, "Your wish will come true."

So the man became the sun. He had the power to warm the earth or to dry it up. And he was very happy. For a while. But one day a cloud passed over him and blocked his powerful rays, and he was very angry. "That cloud is more powerful than I am!" he complained. "Oh, I wish I could be a cloud! *Then* I'd be happy."

And the spirit of the mountain said, "Your wish will come true."

So the stonecutter became a cloud, and he was very happy. For a while. He could make things grow, or he could destroy things by making all the rivers flood. There was only one thing he could not destroy–the huge rocks on the mountainside. This made the cloud angry, and he said, "I wish I were a strong rock on the mountainside. *Then* I'd be happy!"

And the spirit of the mountain said, "Your wish will come true."

So he became a rock on the mountainside. "At last, I am the strongest thing in the whole world!" he said. And he was very happy. For a while. But then one day he heard a strange little noise: *chip, chip, chip, chip, chip*. He wondered what it could be. When he looked down, he saw a stonecutter pounding tools into him. Then a big chunk of the rock went crashing to the ground, and the rock was very angry. "Is this man stronger than I am? Oh, I wish I were a man, so I could be a stonecutter again."

And the spirit of the mountain said, "Your wish will come true." And so the rock became a stonecutter again and worked very hard all day long. He was poor but he was finally satisfied. Never again did he wish to be someone or something else. Never again did he wish to be stronger than everyone else. And he was very happy. For the rest of his life.

GRADES K-3

Choral Reading Read the story aloud and invite the class to play the part of the mountain spirit, reciting the line "Your wish will come true" each time the stonecutter makes a wish.

A Contest Between Sun and Wind In another folktale, the sun and the wind have a contest to see which is stronger. They each try to force a man to take his coat off. Have students predict who would win such a contest and why.

A Wish Come True Have students list things a young person might wish for. Choose one wish, and ask what might happen if it came true. Help them create a story based on the wish.

GRADES 4-6

A Japanese Rock Garden Students will enjoy creating small rock gardens. Bring in a tray and spread sand on the bottom. Gather or buy stones of different shapes, colors, and sizes. Arrange the stones in a pleasing pattern. Add small plants and "lakes" (small foil pans of water).

Rock, Paper, Scissors Invite students to play a folk game that was invented in Japan. Two students put one hand each behind their backs. On signal, each makes the hand sign for rock (a fist), paper (a flat hand), or scissors (two fingers). The stronger sign wins: rock breaks scissors; scissors cut paper; paper wraps rock. If both players make the same sign, it's a tie.

Interviewing the Stonecutter Invite pairs of students to role play an interview between the stonecutter and a news reporter curious about the man's experiences.

Story-Telling Cards

Each card shows how the stonecutter looked at a different part of the story. Cut out the cards and put them in order. Then use them to tell the story to a friend or family member. The first and last cards are alike.

Make a Wish

In July on the holiday called Tanabata Matsuri, Japanese families write their wishes on strips of paper and hang them on bamboo branches. Fill in two wishes on the strips below. The wish list gives you some ideas. Then cut out each wish strip and punch out the hole in each one. Use string or twist ties to hang them on branches.

WISH LIST

strong, big, small, fast,   AS A(N)   tree, ant, bird, mountain,
slow, smart,   airplane, turtle, snail, dancer,
talented, happy, funny   artist, scientist, comedian

THE BEST FOOD IN THE WORLD

Once upon a time, the land of Vietnam was ruled by a wise old emperor who had many sons. The emperor was very tired, but he couldn't decide which of his sons should take over his job. Finally, he had an idea. He called all his sons together and gave them a test. "A year from today," he said, "I will pick one of you to be the next ruler of our country. The prize will go to the one who finds the best food in all the land—but it must be something I have never tasted before."

So all the sons went off to search for the best food in all the land. All except one. Lang Lieu, the youngest son, decided to stay home. He wished he could explore with his brothers, but he had something more important to do. The woman who had taken care of him ever since he was a little boy was now very old and very sick, and Lang Lieu wanted to take care of her. But while he did so, he also thought about what could be the best food in all the land.

Then one night Lang Lieu had a dream. In the dream, an old man spoke to him. "The perfect food in all the world is rice," the old man said. "But you can make a special kind of rice, a rice that is like the heavens and the earth."

The next day Lang Lieu thought and thought about what the old man had said. How could he make rice that was like the heavens and the earth? Well, in those days, everyone believed the earth was square and the sky, or heavens, was a round dome that covered it. Suddenly, Lang Lieu had an idea and ran to the kitchen.

After many months, his brothers returned from their journeys, bringing many wonderful new dishes from all over Vietnam. The emperor tasted each one and wondered how he was ever going to choose the best. At last, he came to his youngest son's dish. Lang Lieu brought some small cakes wrapped in banana leaves. Some of the cakes were round and some were square. They were made of rice with a layer of sweetness in the middle. They were delicious!

"Wherever did you find such a wonderful food?" the emperor said to his youngest son. "You never even left home!"

"I made up the recipe myself," Lang Lieu said, "from a dream I had. The square cakes are to remind us of the sweetness of the earth, and the round cakes remind us of the goodness of the heavens."

"How clever you are, young man!" the emperor said. "And how wise to listen to your dreams! Truly, you are the son I should make the next ruler of the land!"

The emperor named the round cakes *banh day* and the square cakes *banh chung*. And, even today, the people of Vietnam celebrate the New Year with these foods to remind them of the goodness of heaven and the sweetness of earth.

GRADES K-3

Prize-Winning Recipes Invite students to bring in recipes for their favorite holiday dishes and to describe their recipes orally. Publish the recipes in a class cookbook.

The Good Earth and the Good Sky In the story the people remembered the sweetness of the earth and the goodness of the sky. Have students draw pictures that show the good things that the earth and sky give to people.

The Emperor Lang Lieu Ask students what kind of person they would like to have in charge of them (e.g., fair, kind, helpful, smart). Then ask if they think Lang Lieu will do a good job being in charge of his people.

GRADES 4-6

New Year's Customs Have students write descriptions of New Year's customs in their family—either what they do on December 31 and January 1 or how they celebrate religious or ethnic New Year's on other dates.

There's No Place Like Home Many folktale heroes go on long trips to find something special. The hero of this story finds what he's looking for by staying at home. Have students write their own stories about a young person who discovers something special, either by going on a journey or by staying at home.

Dream Work The boy in the story finds the solution to a problem while he is dreaming. Have students read encyclopedias and other books to find out whether it is really possible to solve everyday problems in our dreams.

Crispy Rice Treats

If you have Vietnamese-American friends, ask them to show you how to make *banh day* and *banh chung* out of a special sweet rice and coconut milk. To make a simple treat from crispy rice cereal, try this recipe. It makes about 30 treats.

What You Need:

1 cup peanut butter

2-1/2 cups crispy rice cereal

1/2 cup sugar

2/3 cup corn syrup

large bowl

wooden spoon

What You Do:

1. Mix all the ingredients together in a bowl with the wooden spoon.
2. Use your hands to shape the mixture into balls and squares.
Your crispy rice treats are ready to eat!

Dragons on Parade

In Vietnam and China, the dragon is a symbol of good luck. On the New Year's holiday, people have a dragon parade. Here's how to make a dragon for your own parade.

What You Need:
two sheets of construction paper (two different colors)
scissors
tape
the dragon's head on this page

What to Do:

1. To make the dragon's body, fold each sheet of construction paper in half lengthwise and then fold in half again.

2. Open each sheet. The folds will make four strips on each sheet.

3. Cut out the strips on one sheet and tape them together, end to end.

4. Cut out the strips on the other sheet and tape them together in the same way.

5. Take the end of one long strip and lay it crosswise over the end of the other strip.

6. Now take turns folding one strip over the other until you reach the ends of both strips. Tape both ends together and open the dragon body.

7. Color and cut out the dragon head. Tape it to the dragon body. Now line up with several of your classmates. You can all hold your dragons by the tail end and make them dance as you parade around the room.

HOW THE MICE SAVED THE ELEPHANTS

Long ago in India, there was a town where all the people had moved away. The only creatures left living in all the houses were the mice. But these were very special mice. They put on plays and had wonderful parties and holiday feasts. And they were very happy.

Then one day a herd of elephants came trampling through the mouse town. The elephants were on their way to a lake where there was lots of water for them to drink. Meanwhile, the mice were holding a big party outside that day. When they heard the elephants coming, they squeaked and squealed and scampered for cover, but many of them got hurt.

So the mice held a meeting to decide what to do about this terrible problem. They decided that some of their leaders should visit the elephant king. When the mice found the elephants drinking at the lake, the mouse in charge cleared his throat nervously and then bowed to show his respect for the elephant king.

"Oh, mighty king," he said, "please listen to the problems of some tiny mice. We are small, but we love our little town and our way of living. When you charge through on your way to the lake, you are hurting us, oh mighty king. Would you please think about taking another path to the lake? If you are kind to us, we may have a chance to be kind to you someday, for even the smallest creature can sometimes be of help."

The elephant king thought about the mouse's words. It was hard to believe that such tiny creatures could ever be of help to him, a mighty elephant. "But you never know," he decided. "It could happen." So he agreed to find another path to the lake.

Then one day a human king decided to hunt the elephants by using clever traps made out of ropes tied to trees. Almost all of the elephants stepped into the traps and could not get loose. "Now what can we do?" the elephant king said. "How will we ever get out of this mess?"

And then he remembered his friends, the mice. Maybe they could help. The elephant king sent one of his helpers who had not been trapped into the mouse town to beg for help. And the mice, who had not forgotten the king's favor to them, set out right away to rescue their giant friends.

Thousands of mice used their sharp little teeth to gnaw away at the ropes that had trapped the mighty elephants. And when he was free, the grateful elephant king said, "Now I know for sure:
A friend is a friend no matter how small.
A friend who will help you is the best friend of all."

GRADES K-3

Show and Tell Display photos or drawings of elephants and mice. Have students tell ways they are alike (four legs, tail, color) and ways they are different (size, trunk, etc.).

Walk Like an Elephant Divide the class into elephants and mice and have them act out the story. Elephants can practice walking on all fours, first lifting both left feet and then both right; they can speak in booming voices. Mice can scamper and squeak.

Friends Big and Small Tell students that just as small animals can help big animals, children can help adults. Have them draw pictures of ways they can help adults at home or at school.

GRADES 4-6

True Friends Invite students to write poems about what makes a good friend. They can write rhyming verse like the elephant's lines at the end of the story, or they can use vivid examples to complete the following sentence: "A friend is someone who _____."

Teamwork Works! The mice were able to help the elephants by working together. Invite groups of students to solve problems that require cooperation; for example, how could a group of children of varying ages and sizes work together so that all of them could get over a wall six feet high?

A Herd of Elephants, A Pride of Lions Invite students to research the names used for groups of different animals (*pack* of wolves, *flock* of sheep, etc.). Have them make posters illustrating their findings.

Name_____ Date _____

A Royal Beast

Color the elephant. Then draw a friendly little mouse riding on the elephant's paw.

Elephants at Work Some elephants in India do work for people. What jobs do you think elephants can do? Write some ideas on the lines below.

_____

_____

_____

_____

_____

_____

Name _____ Date _____

Elephant Maze

How many ways can you find for the elephants to get to the lake without going through Mouse Town? Use a ruler to measure each good path. Which way is the shortest?

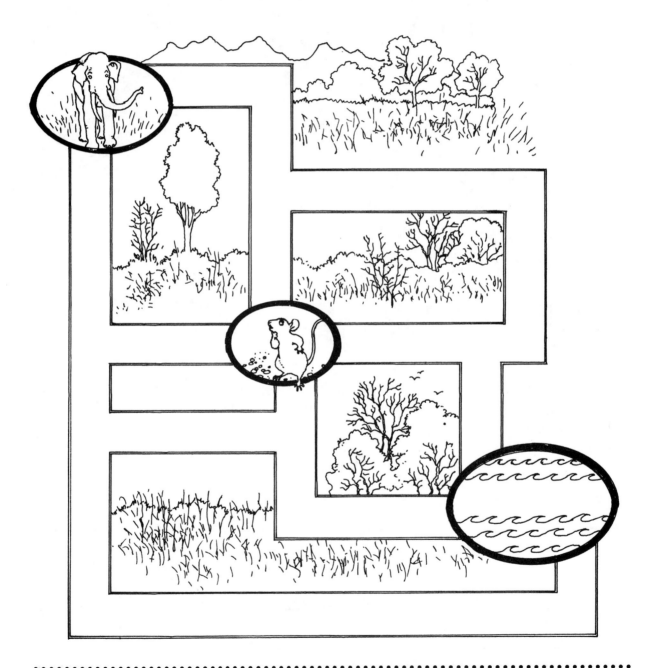

WHY THE TURTLE'S SHELL LOOKS CRACKED

Once there was a turtle who wished he could fly. Now everyone knows that turtles can't fly. But this was the very first turtle in the world, and he could not stop wishing to be like a bird. As a matter of fact, he was best friends with a great bird, the Osprey. Osprey would often come to visit at Turtle's house, and they would have a good time talking and playing games.

Every time he visited, Osprey would say, "Now, Turtle, when are you ever going to come visit me in my house way in the top of the tree?"

And Turtle would say, "I promise I will someday, my good friend, but right now I am just too busy!" Turtle didn't want Osprey to know that he couldn't fly. Turtle's friend Chameleon, the lizard, started teasing him every day. "Hey, Turtle, have you learned to fly yet? Too bad you can't climb trees like me!"

Turtle wished he could avoid his friend Chameleon. But, as you may know, chameleons can change colors and blend into the background, so they're very hard to see from far away. By the time you see them, it's too late to avoid talking to them.

"I wish you'd help me instead of teasing me," Turtle said. And then he thought of a plan for how to get to Osprey's house with Chameleon's help.

The next day, when Osprey came to Turtle's house, Chameleon was there. "I'm sorry Turtle's not home right now," Chameleon said, "but he asked me to give you this present. And he said not to open it until you get home."

"Oh, a present! I love presents!" Osprey said. "I'm going to fly right home and open it. Tell Turtle I'm sorry I missed him."

So Osprey took the package in his beak and began to fly home. Inside the package, as you may have guessed, was a very foolish creature named Turtle, who thought he was very smart for figuring out such a clever way of getting to Osprey's house.

But it took a long time for Osprey to fly home, and after a while Turtle began to get hot inside the package. Very hot. Very, very hot. Finally, he couldn't stand it a second longer.

"Osprey! Osprey!" he called. "Put me down. Get me out of here! Please!"

Osprey was amazed to hear the voice, and he opened his beak to say, "What in the world is that?" And when he did, the package—with Turtle inside—went crashing to the ground. Luckily, Turtle landed on his hard shell, so he did not get hurt. But his shell was cracked all over in a crisscross pattern. And because he was the very first turtle, all the turtles that came later were just like him. That is why, even today, every turtle looks as if it has a cracked shell.

GRADES K-3

Animals Up Close Visit a pet store so that students can observe turtles and chameleons, or invite students with such pets to bring them to school. Have students notice the patterns on a turtle's shell, how hard the shell is, and how a turtle can slide its head and legs into the shell for protection.

Friends Don't Tease! Ask students if Chameleon was being a good friend when he teased Turtle about not being able to fly or climb trees. Ask them to describe other acts that are friendly or unfriendly. Then have them draw pictures showing friendly actions.

Animals in Motion Describe ways that different animals move: *crawl, hop, run, climb, fly, swim.* Have students pantomime the motions. Then display pictures of different kinds of animals. Ask students to pantomime a correct motion for each one.

GRADES 4-6

And That's How It Is Today Invite students to write their own imaginative fables about how an animal came to be the way it is today. Possibilities include the zebra, the giraffe, and the elephant.

Just So Stories After writing fables, students might enjoy reading aloud from Rudyard Kipling's *Just So Stories* (Watermill Classic), which includes "How the Leopard Got His Spots" and "How the Camel Got His Hump."

Cross-Cultural Comparisons Have students compare the moral of this story to the moral of the Japanese story, "The Stonecutter" (pages 12–13). How are they alike? How are they different?

Name _____ Date _____

What Happened Next?

What do you think Turtle and Osprey might say to each other the next time they meet? How would Turtle explain his cracked shell? Would Osprey believe him? Write their conversation on the lines below.

Osprey: _____

_____

Turtle: _____

_____

Osprey: _____

_____

Turtle: _____

_____

Osprey: _____

_____

Turtle: _____

Decorate Turtle's Shell

What You Need:
two paper plates
glue
the patterns on this page
crayons or markers
an 11-inch paper strip

What You Do:

1. Color a turtle-shell design on the bottom of one of the plates. Use any design you like: squares, circles, diamonds, crisscross lines.

2. Color and cut out the head, tail, and leg patterns on this page.

3. Glue the legs onto the inside edge of one paper plate.

4. Glue the head and the tail to opposite ends of an 11-inch strip of paper.

5. Place the head and tail strip between the insides of the two paper plates. Do not glue the strip in place.

6. Glue the two plates together.

7. When you pull the tail, you can slide the turtle's head into his shell, but don't pull it all the way in! Make sure the head still shows so you can pull it back out.

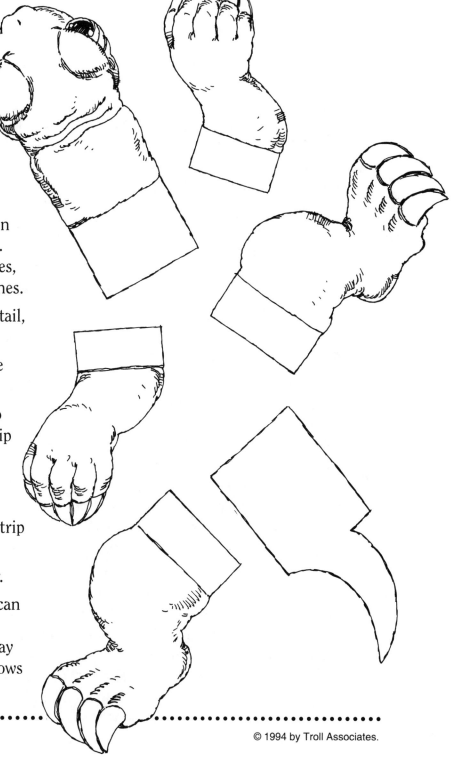

THE HONEY-GATHERER'S SONS

A man in Africa had three amazing sons: The son named Hear could hear the smallest sound from many miles away. The son named Follow could follow anyone's trail for many, many miles. And the son named Fix It could fix anything that was broken or heal anybody who was hurt.

The boys' father was a honey-gatherer. Every day he went on a long hike in the forest to look for honey. He would search and search until he found a tall tree with bees buzzing around it. Then he would know that the bees had made honey in that tree. So he would climb the tree, take the honey home, and eat it.

One day the honey-gatherer found a tall tree with lots and lots of honey in it. He climbed the tree and was reaching for the honey when suddenly the branch he was sitting on broke. Down, down, down, he fell, and he broke his arm.

His son Hear heard the noise and said to his brothers, "Hurry! We must help our father!" Then his brother Follow led the way, and his brother Fix It fixed their father's broken arm.

The next day, the father went out to look for honey again, and his sons stayed home and argued about which one of them was the greatest.

"I am the greatest," said Hear. "You would never even have known that Father was in trouble unless I had heard him fall."

"No," said Follow. "I am the greatest. You would never have been able to find Father without me."

"You're both wrong," said Fix It. "I am the greatest because you would never have been able to fix Father's arm without me."

That day, their father climbed another honey tree and was reaching for the honey when the branch he was sitting on broke. Down, down, down, he fell, and this time he broke his leg.

His son Hear heard the noise, but he didn't tell his brothers because he was angry at them. After a while, when the father did not come home, Follow wondered if something was wrong. But he was too proud to ask if Hear had heard anything. Soon Fix It wondered if something was wrong, but he was too proud to ask Follow to help him find their father.

So the poor honey-gatherer waited and waited for help because his foolish sons were too proud to work together. And that is what always happens, the wise ones say, when people won't admit that they all need each other and that no one is any better than anyone else!

. . . .

GRADES K-3

Sweet Facts Honey is made from a sugary liquid called nectar that is found in flowers. Bees collect nectar with their tongues and start turning it into honey inside their bodies. They store the honey in hollow trees or bee-hives. Visit a beekeeper, bring in honeycombs, display photos of bees at work, or serve honey treats in class.

A Happier Ending Have students act out the story, but change the ending so the brothers learn to work together to help their father.

Super Heroes Unite! Have students bring in pictures or action figures of super heroes and describe the heroes' powers. Ask if any heroes ever work together to help people. For example, how could a hero with super vision help a hero with super hearing?

GRADES 4-6

Tell Me a Story In Africa, storytellers are important people who teach values to children. Have students tell the story, or another one with a moral, to a younger child. Have them practice telling it in words the young child will understand.

Words and Music Like the brothers in the story, songwriters often combine their talents. One person writes lyrics, or words, and another writes music. Invite pairs of students, working together in this way, to write a song about the story.

Rain Forest Treasures Much of the Congo River Valley, where this story takes place, is rain forest. Have students research products and benefits we get from the African rain forest and why the rain forest is in danger.

. . . .

Name _____ Date _____

Find the Honeybees

One of the brothers in the story had super eyes that could follow any trail. How good are your super eyes? Can you find the ten bees hidden in the leaves of the tree? Color them yellow.

Describe a Fourth Brother: What if the three boys in the story had a fourth brother? What super power might he have? How would he use it to help his brothers? Describe the fourth brother and tell what his name is on the lines below.

_____

_____

_____

_____

A Honey of a Banana

You can make a quick treat with three foods that are important in Africa: honey, bananas, and peanuts.

What You Need:

a banana

1 tablespoon honey

1 tablespoon chopped peanuts

a cookie sheet

an oven

What You Do:

1. Have a grown-up heat the oven to 350 degrees F.

2. Leave the banana in its skin. Put it on a cookie sheet and bake for 20 minutes.

3. Have a grown-up remove the banana and cut it in half lengthwise.

4. Pour the honey over the banana halves.

5. Sprinkle the peanuts on top of the honey. Eat out of the skin with a spoon.

ANANSI LOSES HIS POWERS

Long, long ago, a spider-man named Anansi was the only good thinker in the whole world. But he kept the powers of good thinking to himself. He guarded those powers all day long so no one else could be as smart and clever and wise as he was.

Finally, Anansi got tired of guarding his great powers all day. He decided to hide them someplace where no one else could find them. He asked his wife Aso to make a big jar out of clay, so he could hide his powers inside the jar.

Aso found some clay and made a big jar with a very small opening so that Anansi could seal the jar with a stopper and keep all his powers inside. Aso baked the clay jar in the sun until it was dry and strong.

Anansi was very happy with the jar. He pushed all his thinking powers deep inside it and put the stopper in the opening to seal up the jar good and tight. Then he carried the jar into the forest, where he planned to hide it at the top of a tall tree. But Anansi didn't know that his small son Ntikuma was following him and watching his every move.

When Anansi reached the tall tree, he tried to climb it. But he was carrying the big jar in front of him. It hung from a rope around his neck. Every time he tried to climb, the jar got in the way, and he couldn't hold onto the tree. But he kept trying and trying. And soon he was very hot, tired, and angry.

His son Ntikuma was trying to hide, but he couldn't stand watching his father having such a hard time. Finally, he stepped forward. "I have an idea, Father," he said. "Why don't you just tie the jar to your back? Then your hands will be empty and nothing will be in your way. You'll be able to climb the tree easily."

Anansi felt very foolish. He knew that his little son's idea was a good one, but he hated to admit it. He decided to set the jar down on a branch for a while and take a rest so he could think better. But the jar slipped from his hands and went crashing to the ground.

It broke into a thousand pieces. Anansi's thinking powers were carried away by the wind and the rivers until they were spread all over the world.

At first, Anansi blamed his son for the accident and the loss of all his thinking powers. But then he thought about what had happened. "What good did all my powers do me anyway?" he finally said. "My own little son was able to figure out a problem better than I could. Maybe it is better to share my thinking powers with everyone else in the world." And that is just the way the world has been ever since.

. . . .

GRADES K-3

Sound Effects Read the story aloud. Have students make sound effects by playing simple drums made of coffee cans and oatmeal boxes or simple shakers made of tin cans filled with dried beans.

Spiders Are Tricky In Africa there are many stories about Anansi, and he always tries to trick others. Tell students that real spiders are tricky, too. Ask if they know in what way. (Spiders make silk in their bodies and use it to weave webs to trap insects.)

A West African Game On the playground, have students play Big Snake. One student is the snake and chases all the other children. A student who is caught holds hands with the snake. Together, the two of them chase the other children. As each player is caught, the snake gets longer.

GRADES 4-6

Cartoon Tricksters Anansi is a trickster, a character who is always trying to out-smart others. Have students name cartoon characters who are tricksters (Bugs Bunny, Daffy Duck, Road Runner). Then have them draw their own comic strips featuring tricksters.

Ashanti to Yoruba Invite students to research traditional stories, crafts, and clothing of different West African peoples, such as the Ashanti, Ibo, Dogon, and Yoruba.

Spiders: Fact or Fable Many things people believe about spiders are not true. Ask if the following are true or false: Spiders are insects (false). Spiders have eight legs (true). Most spiders are dangerous to people (false).

. . . .

Name _____ Date _____

Make a Clay Jar

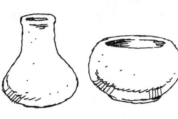

What You Need:
clay
a coffee can
macaroni in different shapes

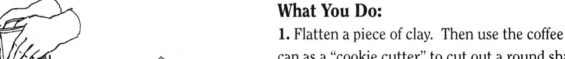

What You Do:
1. Flatten a piece of clay. Then use the coffee can as a "cookie cutter" to cut out a round shape. This will be the bottom of your clay pot.
2. Use the palms of your hands to roll the rest of the clay into ropes about as thick as a pencil.
3. Wind the first clay rope around the edge of the flat bottom you made for your pot. Pinch the rope and the bottom piece together.
4. Now add a new rope by pinching it to the end of the first one. Keep winding the ropes around and on top of the first ones. Continue adding clay ropes until your pot is as big as you want it.
5. Wet your hands and smooth out the bumps on the outside of your pot. Then use your fingernails or push the macaroni shapes into the pot to make designs.
6. Let the pot dry in the sun and the air for a day. Use your pot as a decoration only.

What Will You Keep in Your Clay Pot? Anansi kept his thinking powers in a clay jar. What special things will you keep in your clay pot? Remember, you should not put food or drink in your pots.

_____

_____

GLOOSCAP AND THE BABY

They say that the great warrior Glooscap could outsmart the cleverest magicians and overcome the strongest giants. Glooscap was very pleased with himself. He couldn't help bragging about how powerful he was. Whenever there was a crowd of people around, he would puff out his chest and say in a loud voice, "I am the strongest and smartest person in the whole world. Nobody can defeat me."

After one look at the big strong warrior, everyone in the crowd would agree: Glooscap surely looked like the most powerful person on earth. No one ever challenged him.

Then one day, after Glooscap had been bragging, he thought he heard someone in the crowd laughing. He boomed, "Who dares to laugh at the mighty Glooscap?"

"I'm sorry, sir," a woman said, trying to control her laughter, "but I bet I know someone you cannot conquer or overcome."

"Who is this mighty warrior? Where can I find him?" Glooscap asked in surprise.

"His name is Wasis," said the woman. "But, please sir, I beg you not to try to match wits against him. He will only make you look foolish."

Glooscap was angry. Nobody could make him look foolish. So he asked to be brought to the mighty Wasis at once.

Imagine Glooscap's surprise when he saw the mighty Wasis, for Wasis was just a tiny baby sucking on a piece of maple sugar candy!

"This is the mighty Wasis?" Glooscap laughed. Now Glooscap had been so busy fighting giants and magicians that he had never spent much time with babies. He didn't know much about them.

So he said in a big voice, "Come here, Wasis! Come here now!" The little baby just stared at him and didn't budge an inch.

"Hmm," thought Glooscap. "This might be harder than I thought." Then he had an idea. "This will surely get his attention," he said. He began imitating the song of a bird. But Wasis went right on staring at him and eating his candy. He didn't even crack a smile.

Now Glooscap was angry. "I order you to come here at once!" he said. But the baby kept staring and eating his candy and not budging an inch.

Glooscap tried all the magic spells and songs and chants he had used to overcome his most powerful enemies. But nothing he did could make the baby obey him or even crack a smile.

Finally, Glooscap ran away. He hung his head in shame because he had been beaten at last. As he left, the baby smiled and said, "Goo, goo, goo." And the Algonquians claim that whenever babies say, "Goo, goo, goo," they are remembering a time when one tiny baby overcame the mighty warrior Glooscap.

GRADES K-3

Baby Pictures Have students bring in pictures of themselves as babies and share family stories of what they were like as babies.

Bringing up Baby Ask if any students have a baby brother or sister. Have them describe how they help take care of the baby. What special things do they do to make the baby laugh?

The Mighty Glooscap Have a volunteer play the part of Glooscap bragging about his strength and cleverness. Then have students discuss how they feel about people who always brag about how great they are. Ask when it is okay to brag and when it is not.

GRADES 4-6

Lullaby and Good Night Locate recordings of lullabies used to soothe babies in different cultures. Play the recordings and have students compare and contrast different songs.

Baby-sitter's Guide Have students interview parents about baby-sitting. Then they can write a booklet of tips for when they're old enough to baby-sit.

Name the Baby Contest Tell students that Native American children were often given new names as they revealed new skills or new sides to their personalities. Have students brainstorm new names for the baby in the story. Then have the class vote on the most suitable name.

Make a Native American Buzz Toy

Here is a toy Glooscap could have used to make the baby laugh. It was popular with many Native American tribes. Their buzz toys were made of wood, bone, or stone instead of cardboard.

What You Need:

cardboard
string
scissors 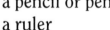 Knot
a pencil or pen
a ruler
the circle pattern on this page

What You Do:

1. Cut out the circle pattern. Trace it on a piece of cardboard.

2. Cut out the cardboard circle. If the cardboard is too thick, ask an adult to help you.

3. Draw two little circles in the center of the big circle. Using a pen or pencil, carefully poke holes through these circles.

4. Measure and cut three feet of string.

5. Pass the string through one hole in the cardboard and then back through the other hole. Tie the ends of the string to form a big loop.

6. Place the cardboard circle in the center of the loop. Hold one end of the loop in your left hand and one end in your right hand.

7. Pull the string tight and twirl it away from you until it is tightly wrapped around itself.

8. Now move your hands in and out, toward each other and then away. Your buzz toy should spin around and make a buzzing noise.

Play a Native American Game

Glooscap might have played this game to relax after losing his contest with the baby. It was played in many Native American tribes.

What You Need:
a plastic bowl
six almonds in their shells
a felt-tip marker

What You Do:

1. Use the felt-tip marker to draw a wide line across one side of each almond.

2. Place the six marked almonds in the bowl.

3. Take turns giving the bowl a slight shake, flipping the almonds, and then catching them again in the bowl.

4. Score one point for each almond that lands with the marked side facing up.

5. Write down your score.

6. Pass the bowl to the next player.

7. After ten tosses each, add up your scores. The player with the highest score wins. Or you can play in two teams of ten players each. Then each player gets one toss.

GRANDMOTHER CORN

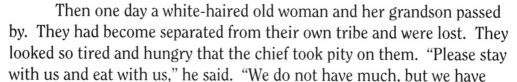

Long ago, the elders say, people did not know how to plant crops. Instead, the men hunted animals for meat, and the women gathered nuts and berries. When times were good, the people ate well, but when there weren't enough animals to hunt, the people went hungry. Even then, though, they worked peacefully together and shared what food they could find, for they had a wise leader who was generous and fair.

Then one day a white-haired old woman and her grandson passed by. They had become separated from their own tribe and were lost. They looked so tired and hungry that the chief took pity on them. "Please stay with us and eat with us," he said. "We do not have much, but we have enough to share."

The white-haired old woman was very grateful. "Your kindness warms my heart," she said to the chief. "And I will do something for you in return. While the mothers and fathers of the tribe are out looking for food, I will watch all the children."

The people agreed. So after the men and women left each morning, the old woman stayed behind to play with the children and tell them wonderful stories. She told about how the mighty god Manitou had made the flowers and the trees and about how other beautiful things had come to be the way they are.

The children loved the stories, but often they would get very hungry as they waited for their parents to return with meat or berries. This made the white-haired old woman very sad. One day she went away for a little while. She came back with a large kettle full of a hot cereal the children had never seen before. It was made from cornmeal. This was in the days before farming, and no one had ever tasted corn. No one except the white-haired old woman knew the secret of corn. And she had decided to share the secret with the people who had taken her in.

When the children tasted the cornmeal cereal, they thought it was delicious. So the old woman began making it for them every day. The cereal gave the children lots of energy, and they grew tall and strong.

But the white-haired old woman was getting older and weaker. One day she said to her grandson, "Soon it will be time for me to go away. But I will leave a special gift for all of you. I have planted seeds of corn nearby. If you and the other children water the plants and sing sweetly to them, the tribe will have plenty of corn in the fall."

The children worked hard in the garden and sang lovely songs about the white-haired old woman as they watered the crop each day. The corn plants grew tall, and the ears of corn grew fat and golden. On the day the corn was ready for picking, the chief called the people together. He said, "The white-haired old woman has gone away forever. But she has left us a very special gift. If we take care of her corn and plant more in the spring, we will never go hungry again."

And now, when the people pick an ear of corn and see the white silk tassels inside, they remember the love of the white-haired old woman who continues to feed them with her gift of corn.

GRADES K-3

Pop Goes the Corn Native Americans first discovered how to make popcorn by dropping corn kernels into a fire. Bring in popcorn kernels. Tell students the kernels are seeds from which new plants can grow. Then make popcorn for the class.

Having a Husking Bee Bring in ears of corn still in their husks. Have students husk them. Point out the silky hair on each ear. Tell students that dried cornhusks can be used to make dolls, mattresses, and brooms.

Corn Songs Tell students that Native Americans used to sing to their corn plants to help them grow. Teach students this Zuñi corn song:

"Nicely, nicely, nicely, away in the east, / the rain clouds care for the little corn plants / as a mother cares for her baby."

(Courtesy Smithsonian Institution Press)

GRADES 4-6

Thank-You Notes Encourage students to think of gifts, attention, and advice they have received from grandparents or other elderly friends. Have them write thank-you notes to these friends or relatives.

Native American Foods Corn is one of many foods Native Americans introduced to European settlers. Have students research what other common foods were first planted by Native Americans.

It's a Corny World To help students appreciate the importance of corn, have them brainstorm a list of things that are made from corn: corn chips, tacos, corn bread, popcorn, cornmeal, corn syrup, cornstarch, corn flakes, corn oil, hominy, grits, etc.

Name _____ Date _____

Enjoying Older Friends

The white-haired old woman played with the children, told them stories, and cooked for them. What do you enjoy doing with a grandparent or another elderly relative or friend? In the box below, draw a picture of yourself and your grandparent or friend doing something together. Then describe the activity in words on the lines.

What We Like to Do: _____

_____

_____

_____

_____

_____

THE NATIVE AMERICAN CINDERELLA

Once there was a great Native American warrior named Strong Wind, who had the power to make himself invisible. Strong Wind lived with his sister by the sea. He wanted to find a good wife, but so many girls wanted to marry him that he couldn't decide which one to choose. Finally, Strong Wind decided to pick the first girl who could see him even when he was invisible. To make sure the girl was telling the truth, he made up a test.

Any girl who wanted to marry Strong Wind had to walk along the beach with his sister. Now usually his sister was the only one who could see him. As Strong Wind came along, his sister would ask each girl, "Can you see him?"

And each girl would lie and say, "Yes, of course."

So the sister would ask, "What is he using to pull his sled?" Some girls would guess a moose hide. Others would say a stick or a rope. But they all guessed wrong, and so Strong Wind knew they were lying.

In the village nearby, there was a chief who had three daughters. The two older daughters were very mean and jealous of their youngest sister. They cut off her beautiful long hair and dressed her in rags. But the youngest sister was always gentle and kind.

The two older daughters both wanted to marry Strong Wind, so they took the test. When his sister asked if they could see Strong Wind, they both said yes. And when she asked what he used to pull his sled, they both said rawhide. So Strong Wind knew the girls were lying and sent them home.

Finally, the youngest sister decided that she would try to see Strong Wind. Her sisters laughed at her and told her she was crazy. But she patched up her clothes with birch bark and went to take the test.

Strong Wind's sister said, "Here comes my brother. Can you see him?"

The girl could not see anyone. Sadly, she spoke the truth: "No," she said. "I cannot see him."

Strong Wind's sister was amazed because the girl told the truth. She tried again. "Are you sure?"

"Oh, now I can," the girl said.

"What is he using to pull his sled?"

"He pulls it with a rainbow," the girl said. And now Strong Wind's sister was really amazed. This girl could see Strong Wind! He must be showing himself to her because she had spoken the truth! Just to make sure, his sister asked, "What is his bowstring made of?"

"It is made of the stars in the Milky Way," the girl answered.

So Strong Wind's sister knew for sure that this girl was meant to be her brother's wife. She took the girl home to her brother's tent and gave her beautiful clothes and jewelry. The girl's shiny black hair grew long again. Then Strong Wind came and asked the girl to be his bride. And ever since then they have done great deeds together.

As for the two mean older sisters, Strong Wind changed them into aspen trees. And today the leaves of the aspen still shake in fear whenever Strong Wind comes along.

• •

GRADES K-3

Sky Riddles Challenge students to guess the answers to silly riddles such as: What kind of bow can never be tied? (a rainbow) What kind of star is not in the sky? (a movie star) Where's the best place to get a milk shake? (the Milky Way)

Little Sister, Big Sister In the story, the two older sisters mistreated their younger sister. Ask how many students are the oldest or the youngest child in their families. Have them discuss the advantages and disadvantages of each position. Then have them make up rules for how big brothers and sisters should treat little brothers and sisters and vice versa.

Make a Rainbow Fill a glass half full of water and place it on a white sheet of paper. Stand outside in bright sunlight or next to a sunny window. Tilt the glass back and forth until a small rainbow forms on the paper. Have students observe and describe the rainbow. Tell them it is caused by light passing through water.

GRADES 4-6

Cross-Cultural Cinderellas Have students compare and contrast this Cinderella to the more familiar European story. How are the characters and events similar? How are they different?

A Modern Cinderella Have students make up their own contemporary stories about a younger brother or sister who is mistreated until he or she wins a great prize that no one else has been able to win.

Sky Facts Have students research sky facts such as how rainbows are formed and why stars shine. Have them illustrate the facts in posters.

• •

Name_____ Date _____

Help the Girls See Strong Wind

Color the picture of Strong Wind holding the rainbow.

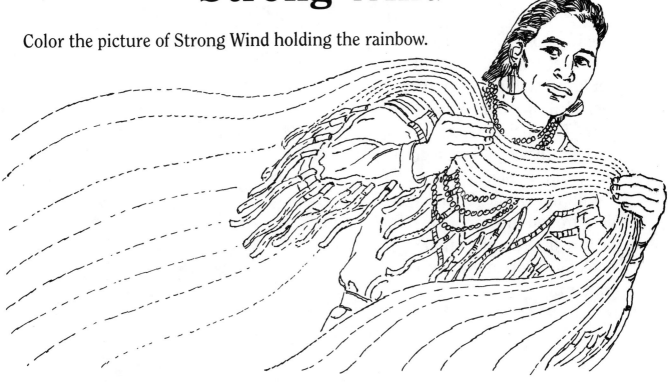

Tell a Rainbow Story: Use your imagination to write a story about how the rainbow colors got into the sky.

_____

_____

_____

_____

_____

_____

Name _____ Date _____

Can You See the Hunter in the Stars?

The Iroquois, Algonquian, and Cherokee tribes all thought they could see pictures when they looked at the stars in the Milky Way. The ancient Greeks also thought they could see a great hunter in the stars. They called the hunter Orion. Connect the dots around the stars to make a picture of Orion the hunter. Look for Orion in the sky on a winter night.

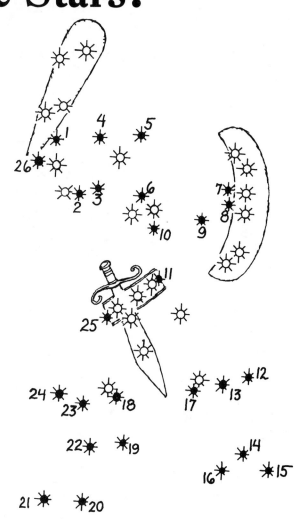

What Have You Seen in the Sky?
Tell about something special you have seen in the sky: a rainbow, a special cloud, stars, lightning, meteors, or anything else.

_____

_____

_____

THE BOY WHO BROUGHT HORSES TO HIS PEOPLE

Long ago, the Blackfoot people on the western Plains did not have horses. Instead, they used dogs to carry heavy loads, and they walked long distances across the Plains to hunt. Now Long Arrow was a boy who was about to become a man. He dreamed of doing something special to make his people proud of him, so he asked his grandfather for help.

"Well," his grandfather said, "I'm not sure I should tell you this. But they say there is a lake where spirit people keep wonderful animals called elk dogs. The elk dogs are bigger than elks and carry heavy loads. They are faster, gentler, and more beautiful than any other animal."

"Oh, I know I can find them!" Long Arrow cried.

"Many young men have tried," his grandfather said, "and not one of them has ever come back."

But Long Arrow was determined to go.

"Before you leave the tipis of your home camp, you must first become a man," his grandfather said.

After Long Arrow became a man, he set off on his journey. He walked for many days and was hungry, cold, and tired. Finally, he came to a giant lake, where he met a small boy in a buffalo skin robe. "Follow me to my grandfather's house," the boy said, and he dove to the bottom of the lake.

Long Arrow was afraid, but he knew he must go. He dove into the water. The spirit magic of the lake helped him to breathe underwater. At the bottom of the lake lived a spirit chief in his spirit tipi. "You are the first one brave enough to dive to my tipi," the chief said. "You may play with my grandson."

The spirit boy took Long Arrow to see the elk dogs. With their long manes and tails and shiny coats, they were so beautiful! Long Arrow jumped on one's back, and it seemed to almost fly over the magical underwater meadow.

The spirit boy said, "If you want to bring some elk dogs home, you must take this test. My grandfather hides his feet under a long buffalo robe. If you can sneak a look at his feet, he will grant you any wish. But I must warn you, it will not be easy. Not even I have ever seen his feet."

For several days, Long Arrow watched carefully each time the old spirit chief went by. But the chief was always careful to keep his feet covered. Long Arrow became very discouraged. Maybe he would never be able to bring the beautiful elk dogs back to his people!

Finally, on the fourth day, Long Arrow watched closely as the spirit chief left his tipi. As the chief walked outside, his long robe caught on the entrance flap of the tipi, and Long Arrow saw what was underneath. Instead of human feet, the chief had elk-dog hooves! Long Arrow gasped in amazement, and the chief turned quickly to face him.

"Well," the spirit chief said, "so you are the one the gods have chosen to learn my secret. What is your wish?"

"Please, sir," Long Arrow said. "I would like to take some elk dogs home to my people."

And so he did. When he returned on the back of an elk dog, the people couldn't believe their eyes. They thought he was a strange new creature, part animal and part man. "It's me! It's Long Arrow!" he said. "I've brought the elk dogs from the spirit world!"

And that is how the Blackfoot people became great riders and hunters of the west, who treasured their elk dogs, or, as we call them, horses.

GRADES K-3

Making Tipis Have students cut out large construction paper circles. Show them how to fold each circle into fourths. Next, cut out and discard one fourth of the circle (see illustration). Students can draw designs on the remainder of the circle. Then fold circles and tape together to form tipis. Arrange the tipis to make a Blackfoot camp.

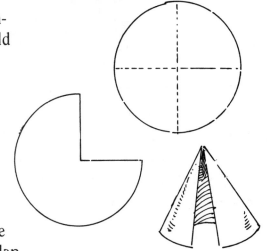

Using Native American Sign Language Native Americans of the Plains spoke many different languages. They developed a common sign language so they could communicate. Teach children this sign for the word *horse:* Have them hold their left hands in front of their chests with the fingers pointing right. Now have them "seat" their right hands "astride" the horse by sliding their left hands between their right index fingers and right middle fingers (see illustration).

GRADES 4-6

Growing up Native American Students who liked this folktale will also enjoy the novel *Jimmy Yellow Hawk* by Virginia Driving Hawk Sneve. It's a story about a contemporary Native American boy who has an adventure with a horse, an experience that helps him grow up. (Available from many libraries.)

How Horses Came to North America Have students research the historical facts about how horses came to North America and became an important part of Native American life. They can make time lines to trace this history.

Name _____ Date _____

Telling a Story in Picture Writing

Many Native Americans wrote stories using pictures instead of words. Below are some pictures they used and what they meant. Use these pictures or make up pictures to draw the story of how Long Arrow brought horses to his people. Draw the story inside the spiral, starting in the center. Keep drawing until you reach the end of the spiral. Then show your picture writing to someone at home and tell the story.

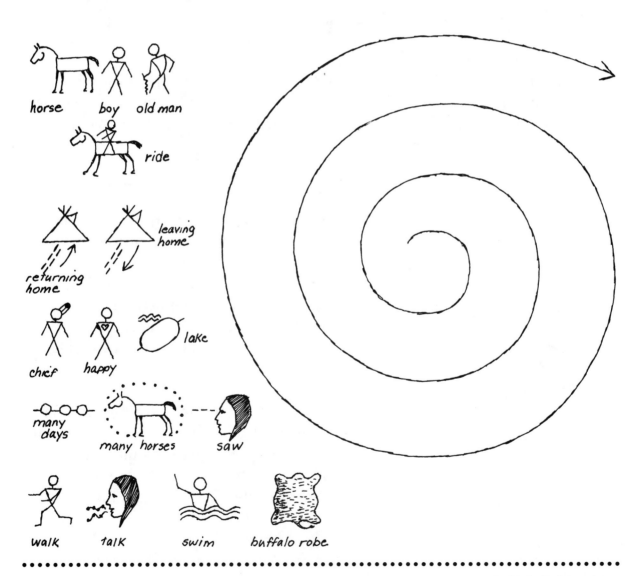

Name_____ Date _____

Native American Horses

Read about two kinds of horses that were popular with Native Americans in the 1800s.
Then color the pictures.

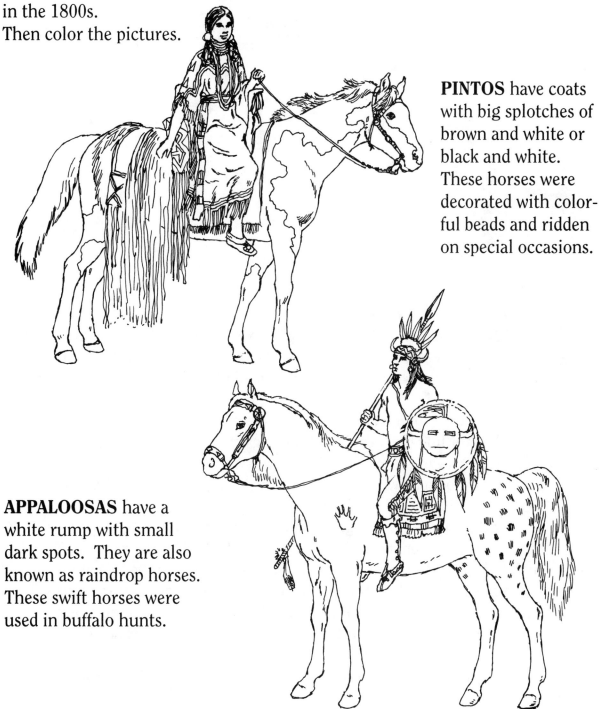

PINTOS have coats with big splotches of brown and white or black and white. These horses were decorated with colorful beads and ridden on special occasions.

APPALOOSAS have a white rump with small dark spots. They are also known as raindrop horses. These swift horses were used in buffalo hunts.

SEÑOR COYOTE AND HIS TAIL

Señor Coyote was a trickster. Sometimes he was very clever. Other times he was very foolish. But he always thought he was the greatest. One day he was taking a walk when two dogs, his enemies, jumped out from behind some rocks and began chasing him.

"I'll just run into the woods," the clever coyote thought. "They'll never find me there." But the dogs were more clever. They blocked his way to the woods so he was forced to run in the open. "There must be somewhere I can hide," he thought. "After all, I am the clever Señor Coyote. No one can outsmart me!"

While he was thinking, two more dogs came running toward him. Now there were dogs ahead and dogs behind. He was trapped. Just then, he looked up at the mountain beside him. On the side of the mountain, he saw a dark hole. Do you know what it was? It was a cave, a place to hide! He made a run for it, huffing and puffing up the mountain. He could hear the four dogs close behind him. Finally, he took one last jump and was inside the cave.

Breathing hard, he waited to see if the dogs would follow. But they were too big to fit through the hole! He was safe! Señor Coyote heard the dogs whining and barking outside. He chuckled proudly, "Oh, I am so clever! I am just too smart for those silly dogs!" Because there was no one around, he began bragging to his own body.

"Hey, feet," he said, "tell me what you did to save me from the dogs."

And do you know what they said? "We ran and jumped and brought you to this cave."

"Gracias," Señor Coyote said. "Hey, ears, tell me what you did to save me from the dogs."

And do you know what they said? "We listened to the dogs barking behind you so you could tell how close they were and so the feet could tell how fast to run."

"Gracias," Señor Coyote said. "Hey, eyes, tell me what you did to save me from the dogs."

And do you know what they said? "We looked out over the rocks and bushes and showed you where to run. We are even the ones who saw this cave."

"Gracias," Señor Coyote said. Then, finally, he turned to his tail. "Hey, you worthless tail, tell me what you did to save me." And do you know what the tail said? Nothing.

"You good-for-nothing tail," Señor Coyote said. "You didn't do anything, did you?"

"Oh yes I did," the angry tail said. "I waved back and forth to the dogs to show where you were. I helped them follow close behind you."

"You traitor!" Señor Coyote screamed. "Get out of here!" And he began backing his tail out the door.

Now the dogs had been listening the whole time. They were waiting with big grins on their faces. When Señor Coyote's tail poked through the door, they grabbed it and pulled the coyote out of the cave. And that is how foolish, clever Señor Coyote was caught by the dogs.

- -

GRADES K-3

Making Predictions Read the story aloud, pausing each time you come to the question "And do you know what they said?" Have students predict what the body parts said. Then read the answers from the story.

Gracias

Thank You Around the World Señor Coyote used the Spanish word *gracias,* meaning "thank you." Teach students how to say thank you in different languages: French—*merci* (mare-see); Japanese—*arigato* (ah-ree-gah-toe); German—*danke* (dahn-kuh).

Coyote Chase Game Draw a mountain on the chalkboard. Make a circle at the top to represent the cave. Draw 20 squares leading to it. Write C for coyote and D for dog at the bottom of the mountain. Students take the parts of "Coyote" and "Dog" and take turns rolling a die to move up the mountain and reach the cave.

GRADES 4-6

Coyote Songs Invite students to write humorous rhyming poems about coyote beginning with these lines: "Coyote is great. He's the smartest of all." Have them read the poems aloud to the class.

A Mexican Fiesta Mexicans celebrate their holidays by holding large parties called *fiestas.* Have students research Mexican foods, games, decorations, and music. Then schedule a fiesta and invite other classes.

The Dog Family Coyotes and dogs are actually cousins. They are also related to wolves and jackals. Have students make illustrated charts comparing and contrasting these members of the dog family.

- -

Name_____ Date _____

Label the Parts of Señor Coyote

Here are the Spanish words for parts of Señor Coyote's body. Using the Spanish words, label each part on the picture.

ear	=	la oreja	**leg**	= la pierna
eye	=	el ojo	**foot**	= el pie
nose	=	la nariz	**tail**	= la cola

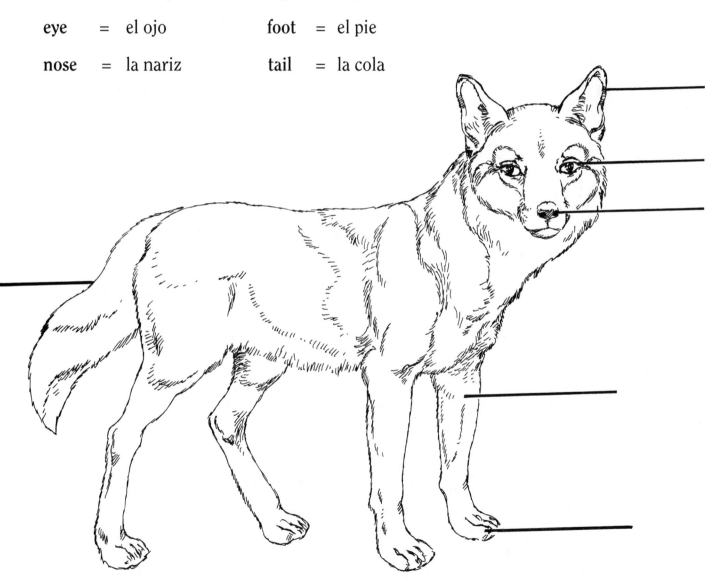

THE BIRD OF SEVEN COLORS

Once there was a servant girl who worked for a cruel master. One day the girl was carrying a pitcher of water. She tripped, and the pitcher broke.

"You clumsy girl," her master said. "That was a very special pitcher. Now you must find the Bird of Seven Colors, for he is the only one who can fix it."

The girl had no idea how to find the magic bird, but she set out anyway. Soon she passed a talking mango tree. "Where are you going?" the tree asked.

"I'm going to find the Bird of Seven Colors so he can fix this pitcher for me," the girl explained.

"If you find him, will you do me a favor?" the tree asked. "Ask him why I have no fruit."

"I promise I'll ask him," the girl said.

She walked for many days and finally came to the ocean.

"Where are you going?" the ocean asked.

"I'm going to find the Bird of Seven Colors so he can fix this pitcher for me," the girl explained.

"If you find him, will you do me a favor?" the ocean asked. "Ask him why I have no fish in my water."

"I promise I will," the girl said.

After many days, the girl reached the mountain where the magic bird lived with his mother, an old woman. When the girl explained her problem, the woman said, "I will try to help, but you must hide from my son. He is magical but also cruel."

Late that night, when the Bird of Seven Colors was asleep, his mother woke him. "My son!" she said. "I need your help! Could you please fix this pitcher?" And he did.

A few minutes later, she awakened him again. "My son! I was just dreaming about a mango tree with beautiful leaves but no fruit. How can this be?"

"There is a treasure chest buried next to its roots," the bird said. "Dig up the treasure and the tree will have fruit. Now let me sleep!"

But the woman had to wake him one more time. "My son! I need to know one more thing! I have heard of a mighty ocean that has no fish. How can this be?"

"Easy," the bird said. "The ocean must eat someone before it will have fish. Now leave me alone!"

The next morning, the girl took her pitcher, thanked the old woman, and went on her way home. When she was almost to the ocean, she called from a distance, "I have the answer to your question. You must eat someone before you will have fish."

"Please come closer and say that," the ocean said, sending out waves to catch her.

"No, I won't," the girl said, and she ran away.

Finally, she reached the mango tree. "There is a treasure buried at your roots," she said. "Someone must dig it up before you can have fruit."

"Will you do it for me?" the tree asked. "You can keep the treasure if you find it."

The girl was happy to help and happy to take all the gold coins she found in the treasure chest. Once she did, the mango tree began to bloom and bear fruit for the very first time.

Now that she was rich, the girl decided not to return to her cruel master. He heard about her good fortune and decided to find the Bird of Seven Colors himself. When he passed the ocean, he was thinking so hard about treasure, he didn't notice a big wave. The wave pulled him into the ocean and swallowed him up. And after that, the ocean always had plenty of fish.

GRADES K-3

Tropical Fruits Find some mangos in a grocery store or specialty foods store. Let students have a taste. Other tropical fruits from Puerto Rico that students might sample are pineapples, coconuts, and oranges.

Birds of Many Colors Have students describe colorful birds they have seen outdoors, in zoos, or on TV. Set up a bird feeder outside your window. Have students observe the birds.

Kind or Unkind? Some story characters were kind, and some were unkind. Have students describe the following characters as kind or unkind: servant girl, her master, Bird of Seven Colors, bird's mother, mango tree, ocean.

GRADES 4-6

Daughter of the Sea and Sun That's the phrase used to describe Puerto Rico in its anthem. On a world map, point out Puerto Rico and the Atlantic Ocean and Caribbean Sea around it. Ask what kinds of activities might be important on this island (fishing, tourism, trade, etc.)

En Español, Por Favor If any students speak Spanish, invite them to retell the story to the class in Spanish. Have the Spanish speaker use gestures and voices to help other students follow along.

Make Your Own Adventure The girl in the story made several decisions that helped decide her fate. Have students reread the story, looking for places where the girl could have made different decisions. Have them rewrite the story showing the effects of different decisions.

Make the Bird of Seven Colors

What You Need:
dried beans in seven colors
scissors
white glue
cardboard
the bird pattern on this page

What You Do:
1. Cut out the bird pattern. Glue it to a piece of cardboard.

2. Spread glue on one part of the bird. Sprinkle on beans of one color and press down. Glue different-colored beans on each part of the bird. Remember to press the beans into the glue.
3. Allow the glue to dry for at least half an hour before you try to pick up your picture.

A Folktale from Costa Rica

THE LUCKY TABLE

Once there was a woman who had two sons. The older son, named Pedro, was very smart. The younger son, named Juan, never stopped to think before he did things. The family was poor. They grew poorer and poorer, until one morning the woman told her sons, "Take our cow to town on market day and sell her!"

On market day Juan and Pedro walked to town. When they got there, the streets were crowded with people selling all kinds of wonderful things—cakes and bananas and tasty tortillas. The boys were very hungry, so Pedro went to buy food.

"Stay here and watch the cow while I am gone!" he said to his younger brother. "Don't talk to anyone!"

As Juan waited with the cow, a boy came along carrying a table on his head. The boy was very clever and decided to play a trick on Juan.

"What a sad looking cow!" the boy said. "I hope you're not trying to sell it. No one will buy it."

"They won't?" said Juan.

"No," said the boy. "But I'll trade you this fine, sturdy table for your cow. Take it or leave it."

"I'll take it!" Juan said.

When Pedro came back, he yelled, "What is the matter with you? Didn't you stop to think? We could have sold the cow for lots of money!"

Sadly, the boys set off for home. Juan carried the table on his head. On the way, they passed through a deep forest. As it was getting dark, they decided to stay there overnight. Because there were pumas in the woods, they decided to sleep in a tree. They took their table with them, so no one would steal it.

Just as they reached the top of the tree, they heard voices below. "Be quiet!" Pedro whispered to Juan. "They might be robbers."

He was right. The robbers came closer and camped under the tree where Pedro and Juan were hiding. They began to count all the money they had stolen.

"Pedro!" Juan whispered. "This table is too heavy! I can't hold it up any longer."

"Shhh!" his brother whispered back. "You have to! If you drop it, they'll know we're here!"

"I'm sorry," Juan said, "I just can't hold it up any longer. I have to let go."

And so he did. The table crashed to the ground right on top of the robbers. The robbers were so surprised and scared that they ran right out of the woods, leaving all the money behind.

Juan and Pedro waited awhile, then climbed down the tree. They collected a rich reward for returning the stolen money. When they finally returned home, they made their mother very happy.

Now isn't it strange how Juan's foolish mistake brought good luck to his family in the end?

• •

GRADES K-3

Juan Went to Town Have students play a memory game about going to market. Ask one student to complete the sentence "Juan went to town and bought a___." The next student repeats the first sentence, and adds a new item to the list. Each student continues to add items.

Swap Day Invite students to bring in inexpensive items they would like to trade. Allow three or four students at a time to go around the room and try to trade their items.

Lucky Linda Tell a simple story about Lucky Linda. Have students identify each lucky or unlucky thing that happens to her. For example, "Linda called her friend, but the friend wasn't home." (Unlucky) "She decided to get the mail and found out she had won a prize at a local store." (Lucky) "But no one could take her to the store." (Unlucky)

GRADES 4-6

Coming Home From the Market It may seem silly to carry a table on your head. But in places where pack animals and vehicles are scarce, people have invented clever ways of carrying things on their heads and backs. Divide the class into groups. Give each group a basket, a doll (representing a 20-pound baby), a large scarf, several potatoes, and a bunch of bananas. Challenge them to figure out the best way one person could carry everything home on foot. (The picture on this page may inspire them.)

News Flash Have students write a news story, complete with headline, based on this folktale.

• •

Name_____ Date _____

Color an Ox-Cart for Juan

Now that Juan has some money, he won't have to carry things on his head or walk everywhere. He can buy an ox to pull one of these beautifully painted ox-carts from Costa Rica. Color Juan and his ox-cart. Draw a picture of what Juan is carrying inside the cart.

THE SEARCH FOR THE MAGIC LAKE

Long ago, in the great Inca empire, there was a prince who became very sick. His father, the emperor, was terribly sad. He said to his people, "I know that the water from the magic lake at the end of the world can save my son. Whoever can fill this golden bottle with water from the magic lake will have all his wishes come true."

Hundreds of brave men tried to find the magic lake, but they all failed. Meanwhile, in a little village, a girl named Sumac was tending her llamas. "Please may I go look for the magic lake?" Sumac asked her parents. "I must save the prince."

"Not our little Sumac!" her mother cried.

But her father said, "We must let her try."

So Sumac set out with one of her llamas to keep her company and carry her food. But there were pumas in the woods, so Sumac sent her llama home to safety. She slept in a tree and hid her food in the tree trunk where the pumas could not get it, but the little birds could share it with her. The next morning the birds awakened her. "Thank you for sharing your food, little girl. Now we would like to help you." Each bird pulled out one of its feathers and gave it to Sumac. "Hold these together and they will make a magic fan. It will protect you and take you anywhere you want to go," they told her.

Sumac held the fan and said, "Take me to the lake at the end of the world." And, suddenly, there she was on the shore of the most beautiful lake she had ever seen! "But I didn't bring anything to put the water in!" Sumac realized. "Now what will I do?"

Just as she said that, the emperor's golden bottle magically appeared at her feet. Sumac picked it up and ran to dip it in the magic lake. But a horrible voice stopped her. It said, "Get away from my lake, you foolish girl!" She looked up. There was the scariest creature she had ever seen—a giant flying snake with flashing red eyes. Sumac was shaking with fear, but she knew she could count on her magic fan to protect her. One wave of the fan and the snake vanished in a puff of smoke.

Sumac filled the golden bottle and then waved her fan again. "Take me to the palace," she said.

At the palace, a guard stopped her. "Now where do you think you're going, little girl?"

"I have the magic water!" Sumac said.

The guard smiled, not believing her—until he saw the golden bottle. "Come right in!" he said.

When the prince drank the magic water, he was instantly well again. "Tell me your wishes," the emperor said to Sumac. "They will all come true."

"I have only one," said Sumac. "Please give my parents a nice farm with plenty of llamas, so we will always have lots of warm wool."

"That's all?" the emperor said. "Wouldn't you like to stay here in the palace with us?"

"Oh, no," said Sumac. "All I want is to go home to my family and my llamas." And that is what she did.

GRADES K-3

Lovely Little Llamas   Llamas are smaller than camels and have no hump. Like camels, they are beasts of burden and can go for days without food or water. In fact, llamas were once called "little camels of the Andes." Have students explain another name for llamas: "trucks of the Andes."

Animals and People   Sumac's llama helped the family by carrying supplies and providing wool. In return, Sumac protected the llama. Ask if students have animals at home. What do the animals do for them? What do they do for the animals?

The Home of Chocolate   Chocolate comes from *cacao* beans, first grown in South America. Bring in unsweetened cocoa for students to taste the bitter powder. (Be sure no one is allergic to chocolate.) Follow the recipe on the can to make hot chocolate, or use chocolate syrup to make cold chocolate milk.

GRADES 4-6

The Inca Empire   Although they had no written language and had not invented the wheel, the Inca built an empire in South America. Llamas helped them by carrying supplies to build roads and temples and by providing wool, meat, leather, and rope. Have students research the ancient "lost" Inca city of Machu Picchu. Listen to recordings of Andean music from your public library.

The Hero's Journey   Many folktale heroes make journeys to find something precious for themselves or others. Have students compare and contrast Sumac's journey with those in "The Bird of Seven Colors" (page 64) and "The Boy Who Brought Horses to His People" (page 55).

Make an Award

Do you think Sumac deserved an award for her bravery? Do you know someone else who has done something to deserve an award? Color the award below. On the lines fill in the name of the person who will receive the award and tell what the person did to deserve it. Then cut out the award and present it to the brave person. (You could even roll it up and tie a ribbon around it.)

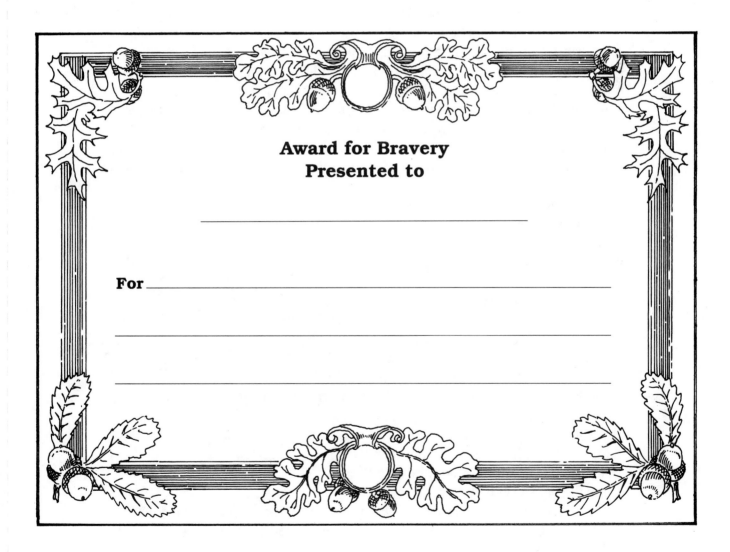

Award for Bravery
Presented to

_____

For _____

_____

_____

A Creole Folktale from the Southern United States

THE TALKING EGGS

Once there were two sisters named Blanche and Rose who lived on a farm with their mother. The girls' father had died when they were small, and there was more than enough work on the farm to keep a woman and two girls busy. The trouble was, Blanche, the younger sister, had to do most of the work because her mother and her older sister, Rose, were so lazy and mean.

One day the mother told Blanche to go to the well and bring back some water. At the well, Blanche saw an old woman in worn-out clothes who asked for a drink. "Of course," Blanche said. "Take all you need." "You're a good girl," the old woman whispered. "And I'll never forget your kindness."

When Blanche returned home, her mother scolded her because the water was too warm and sent her back for more. Tired of being treated unfairly, Blanche decided to run away from home. She didn't know where to go, until, suddenly, she saw the old woman from the well.

"Don't cry, little girl," the old woman said. "You can come to my house for supper, but first you must promise not to laugh—no matter what you see."

Blanche gave her promise, but she had no idea how hard it would be to keep. When they got to the old woman's house, the first thing she saw was a two-headed cow with twisted horns. Then the cow opened its two mouths and went "hee-haw" just like a donkey! And in the yard, chickens with blue feathers hopped around on four feet! Blanche really wanted to laugh, but she remembered her promise. And, besides, she didn't want to hurt the old woman's feelings.

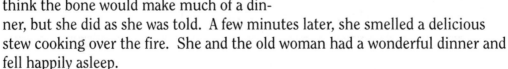

When they got inside the house, the woman handed Blanche a dry old bone and asked her to boil it for dinner. Blanche was very hungry, and she didn't think the bone would make much of a dinner, but she did as she was told. A few minutes later, she smelled a delicious stew cooking over the fire. She and the old woman had a wonderful dinner and fell happily asleep.

The next morning, the old woman said, "Out in my chicken coop are some magic talking eggs. Go out and gather some, but only the ones that say, "Take me." On your way home, throw the eggs over your left shoulder, and you'll see a surprise."

Out in the chicken coop, Blanche saw some eggs that looked normal and others that were covered with jewels. All of the normal eggs said, "Take me! Take me!" But all of the eggs with jewels cried, "Don't take me! Don't take me!" Blanche was disappointed that she couldn't have any of the fancy eggs, but she did as she was told. Then she thanked the old woman, said good-bye, and headed for home.

On her way, she threw eggs over her left shoulder, and, one by one, out popped diamonds and coins and fancy dresses. And out of the last egg sprang a beautiful horse and cart, which Blanche rode home in.

When her mother and sister saw her, they demanded to know where all the beautiful things had come from. And the next morning, Rose, the mean older sister, set off to get more riches.

When she met the old woman in the woods, she said, "I surely would like to see your house, m'am."

"Okay," the old woman said, "but you must promise not to laugh—no matter what you see."

Rose promised, but as soon as she saw the two-headed cow and the blue chickens, she burst out laughing. The old woman just shook her head.

At dinner time, the old woman gave her a dry bone to boil, and Rose said, "Are you crazy? What kind of dinner is that?" And so they went to bed hungry.

The next morning, the old woman sent Rose out to the chicken coop, telling her exactly what she had told Blanche. But, of course, greedy Rose could not resist the beautiful eggs with jewels on them, even though they said, "Don't take me! Don't take me!" She grabbed them all and ran for home without even saying thank you or good-bye to the old woman.

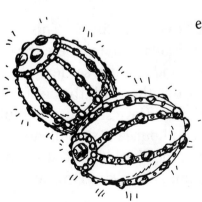

On her way home, she began throwing the eggs over her right shoulder, and do you know what came out of them? Snakes and toads and hornets and a mean hungry wolf all began chasing Rose home. Her mother tried to rescue her, but the creatures only started chasing her, too. By the time Rose and her mother were able to escape and return home, Blanche had gone off to the city to live the good life she deserved. As for Rose and her mother, they kept searching every day to find the old woman and her magic eggs again, but they never did.

• •

GRADES K-3 ——————————————————

Magic Eggs Blanche's kindness and good behavior were rewarded with gifts from the magic talking eggs. Bring in your own "magic" eggs—egg-shaped pantyhose containers or plastic Easter eggs that screw together. Place little treats inside the eggs, and give one to each student. Or use the eggs as prizes in games or rewards for other achievements.

Good Manners When visiting the old woman, Blanche respected the woman's feelings and behaved politely. Have students role-play polite ways to act when they are guests or hosts in each other's homes. Include situations such as sharing food and toys, obeying rules, and respecting the property of others. Students might enjoy hearing the book *Manners,* by Aliki (Greenwillow, 1990) read aloud.

GRADES 4-6 ——————————————————

Further Adventures of Blanche and Rose Tell students that in different versions of this story, Blanche and Rose see additional strange things at the old woman's house. Have students imagine other things the girls might see and how each girl might react to them.

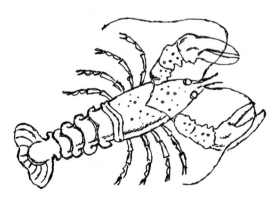

Louisiana: A Feast of Cultures This story was told in Louisiana, a state where the cultures of French and Spanish settlers (Creoles) came together with the cultures of African Americans. Have students do multimedia reports on Louisiana's Cajun and Creole cooking, the Mardi Gras festival, and jazz, blues, Cajun, and zydeco music.

• •

Name_____ Date _____

The Old Woman's Amazing Animals

Color the old woman's two-headed cow and four-legged chicken. Then draw another strange animal that might have lived on the old woman's farm.

THE PRINCE WHO LOVED MUSIC

Long ago, the czar, or emperor, of Russia had two beloved daughters named Sonia and Sophia. But one sad day, a magic whirlwind came and took them away. The czar and his wife, the czarina, were very unhappy.

Time passed, and the czar and czarina had a son named Feodor. He was very strong, but he hated to fight. Instead, he loved to play music, especially a stringed instrument called the balalaika. Whenever he played a happy tune, people couldn't help but dance.

But the czar was disappointed in him. "If you will not fight," he said, "who will defend my kingdom?"

"Father," said Feodor, "a good brain can defeat the strongest arm and the sharpest sword. I will prove it. I will go and find my two sisters who were taken by the magic whirlwind."

The czar admired his son's courage, but he begged Feodor not to go.

"I will find my sisters," said Feodor, "and I will bring them home." So he set off, carrying only his balalaika. He walked for many days until he came to a deep forest where the earth trembled and went *boom! boom! boom!* Suddenly, Feodor came upon two giants fighting, using huge trees as weapons!

Feodor was scared. He took out his balalaika and began to play. Before long, the mighty giants were dancing and singing. When they had to sit down and rest, the prince spoke up.

"What are you fighting about?" he said.

"We are fighting over the most amazing treasures in the world," one

giant said. "A magic cloth that makes wonderful feasts appear, a magic hat that makes its owner invisible, and magic boots that can go ten miles in a single step."

"I must have those things," Feodor thought. So he said to the giants, "Why don't you both start running down that path? The first one who passes the other will win the treasures." When the giants started running, Feodor grabbed the treasures. He put on the magic boots and was soon far, far away.

Finally, he came to the house of an old woman who lived all alone in the woods. "Excuse me, old woman," the prince said. "I am looking for two princesses named Sonia and Sophia. Do you know where they are?"

"Ah," the old woman said. "They are prisoners in the white palace of the King of the Forest. I can show you the way, but you'll never make it back alive."

Feodor gulped in fear, but he tried to sound brave. "I'll make it. Don't worry," he said. And his magic boots took him to the white palace.

When he arrived and introduced himself, his sisters gave him a big hug. Then Sonia said, "You must hide! The King of the Forest is coming!" And Sophia said, "If he catches you, he will surely eat you!" And just then a huge gust of wind blew through the walls and shook the whole palace. So Feodor put on his magic hat and disappeared.

But the King of the Forest smelled Feodor and said, "Where is that tiny prince? I want to eat him."

Feodor spoke up and said, "I have a better idea, your majesty." He spread the magic cloth, and a tremendous feast appeared, with twelve servants to wait on the king. Feodor and his sisters watched nervously as the king stuffed himself for hours. Would they ever have a chance to get away? Then, after his fifth dessert, the King of the Forest finally heaved a sigh and fell into a deep, deep sleep.

"Hurry!" Feodor said to his sisters. "Jump on my back!"

"But how can you carry us all the way home?" Sophia said. "It will take days, and we will surely starve on the way!" Sonia said.

"Don't worry," Feodor answered. "My magic boots will have us home in a flash!" And they really did.

The czar and czarina were amazed. At last their family was together again! And their noble son Feodor had done it all without using a lance or a sword—only his brain and his balalaika.

• •

GRADES K-3

Russian Nesting Dolls Wooden dolls of different sizes that fit inside each other are a favorite toy in Russia. Your students can make their own version with different sizes of foam or paper cups. Have them use felt-tip markers to draw a giant on the side of the largest cup, the King of the Forest on the next largest, and Prince Feodor on the smallest. Show them how to nest the toys inside each other.

Playing a Russian Game Take the class outside or to the gym to play czars. Choose one student to be the czar. Have the others pick an action to pantomime for the czar. If the czar guesses the action being pantomimed, the students run and the czar tries to tag them. The first student tagged is the next czar.

Great Russian Music One of Russia's most famous composers was Peter Ilyich Tchaikovsky. Children may enjoy listening to selections from his famous work, "The Nutcracker Suite," while you read a picture book version of the story.

GRADES 4-6

A Book of Giants Students who like fantasy will enjoy the clever illustrations and traditional stories in the book *Giants* by David Larkin. You can find it in the folklore section of your library.

The Mysterious Balalaika Locate pictures of this stringed instrument and play recordings of balalaika music for the class. Have students compare its sound to that of other stringed instruments, such as the mandolin or guitar.

• •

A Folk Song from Eastern Europe

Listen as your teacher plays or sings "Morning Comes Early" for you. Then sing it with your classmates. You can even sing it as a round. Divide into two groups. The first group sings "Morning comes early and…" As they begin the next word, "bright," the second group starts the song from the beginning. Good luck!

STEALING THE MOON

Everyone knows that some people can be very foolish sometimes. But did you ever hear of a town where *all* of the people were foolish *all* of the time? That's how it was in the village of Chelm, where people did one foolish thing after another from morning to night. Why, the people of Chelm were so foolish that they even tried to steal the moon. This is how it happened.

In those days, there were no electric lights. When night came, it was very, very dark outside. "Oh, I wish there was some way we could go out at night without getting lost or bumping into each other," said a young man of Chelm.

"There is," said an elder with a long white beard. "All we have to do is steal the moon."

"Steal the moon!" the people cried in amazement.

"Yes," said the elder. "Did you ever notice that during that part of the month when the moon is shining bright we can see all night long? But then the moon goes away for part of the month and leaves us in the dark. Is that fair?" He didn't wait for them to answer. "If we steal the moon, it will have to shine for us every night."

"Oh, he is so wise!" said one of the young women of Chelm. "But how will we do it?"

"Simple," said the elder. "All we do is wait until a night when the moon is full and bright. Then we bring out a barrel of water and wait until we can see the moon inside the barrel. Then, quick as we can, we cover the barrel with a burlap bag and trap the moon inside!"

And that is just what they did. Once they had captured the moon in the barrel, they brought it inside the synagogue, the special building where they prayed and held meetings. They guarded it carefully for two weeks, until the nights became very dark again.

"It's time to bring out our moon and hang it in the sky," the elder said. Everyone gathered around to watch the great event. All of the people held their breath as they waited for the moon to be taken out of the barrel. They put their hands loosely over their eyes so they would not be blinded by the light. They got more and more excited as the burlap was slowly removed from the barrel, until there was…nothing! The moon was gone! It had escaped—or been stolen! But who would have dared to take their moon? And how did they get it out when it had been so carefully guarded? It was a very great mystery indeed.

"A guard must have fallen asleep one night," the elder said. "We must be more careful the next time. We will try again in two more weeks when the moon is full again."

All of the people of Chelm nodded their heads and thought how lucky they were to have such a wise leader. They could hardly wait to steal the moon again.

GRADES K-3

Nighttime Scenes Invite students to make pictures showing a moonlit scene. Have them start with a sheet of black construction paper to represent night. Glue on a white circle or crescent shape for the moon. Glue on tiny pieces of foil for stars.

Students can cut out or draw other shapes to make people, buildings, and animals. They can then tell stories about their pictures.

Counting by Moons Tell students that it takes the moon one month to go from new (or invisible), to full, to new again. Long ago, many groups of people used the changes in the moon to measure time. The time from one full moon to the next was called *one moon*. In fact, our word *month* comes from the word *moon*. Invite students to describe amounts of time using moons instead of months. For example, how many moons away are their birthdays or vacations?

GRADES 4-6

Mavens and Mensches The Jews of Eastern Europe spoke *Yiddish*, a mixture of German, Hebrew, and Slavic languages. Many Yiddish words have entered English. In a good dictionary, have students look up the following words and then act them out: *schmoose, nosh, schlep, kibitz, schmaltz, chutzpah, mensch, maven.*

Phases of the Moon Have students research why we see phases of the moon. They can then observe the night sky and fill in the moon calendar on page 88.

More Tales of Chelm For more tales of the people of Chelm, students may enjoy reading *Zlateh the Goat and Other Stories* by Isaac Bashevis Singer (HarperCollins, 1966).

two mensches schmoosing

Play a Dreidel Game

During Hanukkah Jewish children play with a special kind of top called a *dreidel* (dray-dul). You can make your own dreidel and play a game with it.

What You Need:
the dreidel pattern on this page
construction paper
scissors
a pencil
dried beans for keeping score

What You Do:
1. Trace the dreidel pattern onto a square piece of construction paper. Remember to include the lines, the Hebrew letters, and the English words for each letter. Cut out the dreidel.
2. Poke a pencil through the center of the dreidel to make your top.
3. Give ten dried beans to each player.
4. Take turns spinning the top. Watch how it lands. If it lands on "take five" or "take ten," take that many beans from the person on your left. If it lands on "nothing," you take no beans. If it lands on "lose one," give one bean to the person on your left.
5. Give each person five chances to spin the dreidel. The players then count their beans. The person with the most beans wins the game.

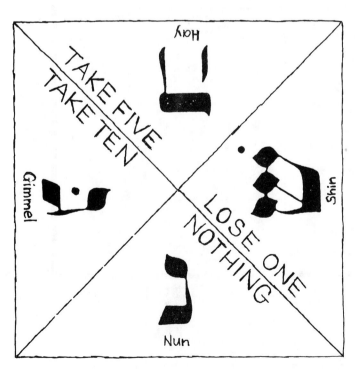

Name _____ Date _____

Make a Moon Calendar

Make a moon calendar using the blank calendar below. First, fill in the name of the month and the dates. Then check a daily newspaper to find out when the new moon, first quarter, full moon, and last quarter will appear. Cut out the moon shapes on the bottom of the page. Paste them on the correct dates. Then watch the night sky to see if you can spot each shape on the correct date.

_____
Name of Month

SUNDAY	MONDAY	TUESDAY	WEDNESDAY	THURSDAY	FRIDAY	SATURDAY

THE UNLUCKY SHOES

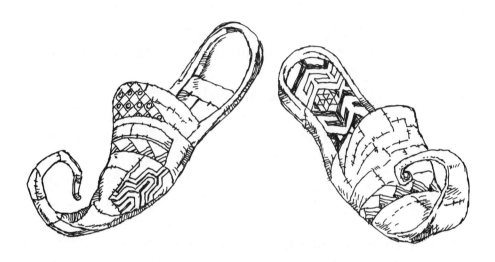

Long ago, there lived in Baghdad a rich man named Ali Abou. Even though he was rich, Ali hated to spend money. People said he had worn the same pair of shoes for many years because he did not want to buy new ones. Whenever he got a hole in the shoes, he would take them to a shoemaker and get them patched. Over the years, he had collected patches of many colors until his worn-out shoes began to look like a walking rainbow. Everyone pointed and laughed when he walked by, but he didn't care—until the shoes brought him bad luck.

It all started when Ali Abou went to the public baths, which were like the public swimming pools of today. His old friend Omar looked at his shoes and said, "Those shoes are terrible! When are you ever going to get some new ones?"

Ali paid no attention. He slid the shoes under a bench and went into the baths. But when he came out, his shoes were gone! Instead, there was a brand-new pair where his old ones had been. "Oh, that rascal Omar," Ali thought. "He has gone out and bought me some new shoes. How kind!" So he slipped on the new shoes, which were just his size.

But his old shoes were still under the bench. Omar hadn't bought him new shoes at all. The new shoes really belonged to the judge of Baghdad! When the judge found that his shoes were missing, he was very angry. "What thief dares to steal the shoes of the judge of Baghdad?" he shouted. And there, under the bench, were the worn-out, rainbow-patched old shoes of Ali Abou. "Bring that rich old thief to me and throw him in jail!" the judge roared.

So Ali Abou went to jail. When he finally got out, he decided to get rid of the old shoes that had caused him so much trouble. He began digging a hole in his garden to bury them in. But the hole was right next to the wall that divided his garden from his neighbor's. When the neighbor heard the noise, he said, "I know what you're doing, Ali. You're digging a hole to my garden and planning to rob me. Wait until the judge hears this!"

When the judge saw Ali Abou in his court again, he said, "Haven't you learned your lesson?" And he threw Ali in jail. When Ali got out of jail, he tried to get rid of the shoes again. He threw them in the sewer. But the shoes clogged up the sewer pipe, and soon he was back before the judge.

This time Ali Abou held up his shoes and said, "Judge, it is these shoes that deserve to go to jail. Please lock them up and get them out of my sight."

The judge looked at him as if he were crazy, but he asked Ali Abou to continue. As he heard Ali's story, the judge couldn't help smiling. Then he laughed and laughed until he cried. "Don't worry, Ali Abou," the judge finally said. "I will take care of your wicked shoes. They will never bother you—or anyone else—again." And that was the last that was ever seen of Ali Abou's unlucky shoes. No one was ever able to find out what the judge had done with the poor shoes. What do *you* think?

THE UNLUCKY SHOES
CLASS ACTIVITIES

. . . .

GRADES K-3

Old Shoes, New Shoes Have students share stories of getting new shoes and breaking them in or of old shoes they outgrew but hated to give up. Have them draw pictures of their favorite pairs of shoes and tell why they like them.

Stories from the Land of Aladdin
Many students are probably familiar with the story "Aladdin." Tell them this story comes from the same country as the "The Unlucky Shoes." Read aloud picture book versions of "Aladdin" and other stories from *The Arabian Nights* about Ali Baba and Sinbad the Sailor.

Pita Bread Snack Flat breads like pita bread are traditional in the Middle East. Prepare a Middle Eastern snack by toasting pita bread. Spread it with peanut butter or with *hummus*, a Middle Eastern spread made from chickpeas and sesame paste.

GRADES 4-6

Multicultural Shoes Students can explore shoes worn in different cultures, such as Native American moccasins, the wooden shoes of Holland, and the Arabian curled toe shoe featured in this story. Have them compile a scrapbook illustrating different shoes. They can describe how climate, available materials, and beliefs influenced people's footwear.

Arabic Numerals Tell students that our system of arithmetic—using the Arabic numerals 1-10 and the decimal system—was developed in Baghdad around 800 A.D. Teach them Roman numerals. Have them compare adding 448 and 337 using Arabic and then Roman numerals.

. . . .

Name _____ Date _____

Color Ali Abou's Shoes

Color the rainbow patches on Ali Abou's shoes. Then tell what you would have done to get rid of the shoes if you were Ali Abou.

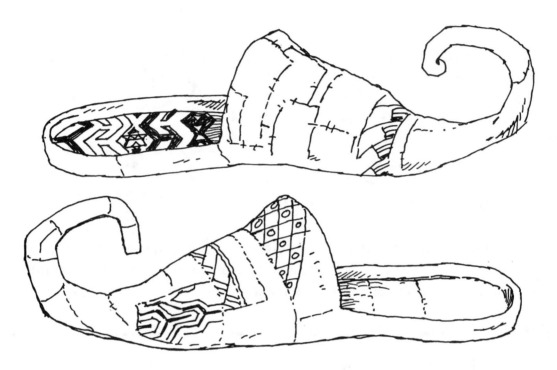

How I would have gotten rid of the shoes:

_____

_____

_____

_____

_____

_____

A Folktale from the South Pacific

KOKOA LEARNS THE SECRET OF FIRE

Long, long ago, before people had learned to make fire, they couldn't cook their food. They had to eat it raw. Now people in the Pacific Islands were surrounded by volcanoes. Sometimes they could even cook their fish and sweet potatoes in the fiery lava from the volcanoes. "Ah," they would say, as they tasted a roasted sweet potato, "if only we could eat like this all the time!" They still did not know the secret of making a fire whenever they wanted.

Finally, the chief of one island offered a reward to anyone who could discover the secret of making fire. Many young people tried, but they soon gave up. But one boy named Kokoa refused to give up. Luckily, he had his wise old grandmother to help him. She told him, "Find the mud hens, Kokoa, and you will learn the secret of fire. I have seen them cooking sweet potatoes out by the pond."

So do you know what Kokoa did? He went out to the pond where the mud hens lived. He hid in the reeds along the shore. Soon he heard the hens chirping, and he looked up to see them gathering sticks.

"This will be easy. I'll just watch," he said. But he couldn't see much from his hiding place. He knew that the hens gathered dry sticks, but he couldn't see what they did with them.

That night, when he told his grandmother what had happened, she said, "You must sneak up on them and get a better view."

So do you know what Kokoa did? The next day, while the hens were busy roasting potatoes, turning them carefully so they would cook just right, Kokoa sneaked up and caught a bird. The other birds flew away, squawking, "Don't tell the secret!"

"Please let me go. Please!" the bird chirped.

"I will if you tell," Kokoa said.

"Well..." the bird began slowly, "all you need is a stick from a softwood tree and a root from the taro plant. Just rub them together and the magic happens."

And do you know what Kokoa did? He tried doing what the little bird said—but he held on tight to her just in case she was lying. He was smart to do that, because no fire started. "You lied to me!" he said.

"Oh, I'm sorry," said the bird. "Did I say taro root? I meant you should use a banana stem."

But Kokoa could tell she was lying again. "Tell me the truth or I will never let you go!" he said.

And, finally, the little bird gave up. "Take a softwood tree stick and rub it against a stick of the hardest tree in the forest."

So Kokoa did. And do you know what happened? After a while, a little puff of smoke came out. After a while longer, a flame flared up. Kokoa tended the fire patiently. Very slowly, he was able to roast a potato. It tasted so delicious that he decided to roast another one before taking the secret back home. And ever since then, people have said that food cooked outdoors over a fire is the best food of all.

• •

GRADES K-3 ─────────────────────

Making Predictions Read the story aloud. Pause each time you come to a question such as, "So do you know what Kokoa did?" Have students predict the answer. Then continue reading so that they can verify their predictions.

Cookout Memories Have students share stories about camping trips or outdoor barbecues with families and friends. What special foods did they cook?

GRADES 4-6 ─────────────────────

If At First You Don't Succeed In order to succeed, Kokoa had to keep trying despite moments of failure and frustration. Have students write about trying and failing before they learned to do something new, such as swimming, playing baseball, or playing an instrument.

The Ring of Fire Hundreds of volcanoes encircle the Pacific Ocean in a wide band called the Ring of Fire. These volcanoes formed where the plates that cradle the Pacific meet the plates that hold the continents. Have students research volcanoes in encyclopedias and geography books to find out more about the Ring of Fire and what makes a volcano erupt.

The Gift of Fire The story focuses on people's desire to cook food. Have students brainstorm other ways that learning how to make fire helped people (providing warmth, light, protection, etc.).

• •

My Favorite Foods

What foods do you like to eat cooked? What foods do you like to eat raw? What foods do you like to eat either raw or cooked? Cut out the pictures and paste them in the boxes below. Then compare your food chart with those of your classmates. Did you pick the same foods?

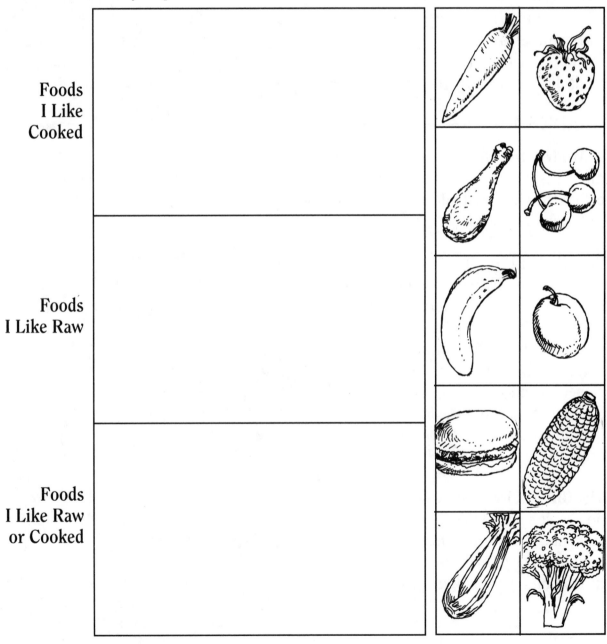

Foods I Like Cooked

Foods I Like Raw

Foods I Like Raw or Cooked